Windows and a Looking Glass

New Women's Voices Series, No. 127

poems by

Deborah Kahan Kolb

Finishing Line Press
Georgetown, Kentucky

Windows and a Looking Glass
New Women's Voices Series, No. 127

Copyright © 2017 by Deborah Kahan Kolb
ISBN 978-1-63534-171-3 First Edition
All rights reserved under International and Pan-American Copyright Conventions.
No part of this book may be reproduced in any manner whatsoever without written permission from the publisher, except in the case of brief quotations embodied in critical articles and reviews.

ACKNOWLEDGMENTS

I would like to thank the editors of the anthologies and magazines in which the following poems first appeared:

Veils, Halos & Shackles: "Eldest Daughter"
Voices Israel 2015: "After Auschwitz," "Monthling"
Poetica: "Zhou Ling" (Finalist for the 2014 Anna Davidson Rosenberg Poetry Award)

I am grateful to Charles Fishman, whose discerning edits helped reshape "Eldest Daughter," and to Sharon Olds, whose early insights and critiques made it possible for some of the poems included in this volume to reach their potential.

Publisher: Leah Maines

Editor: Christen Kincaid

Cover Art: Renee Dvir

Author Photo: Maxx Eisner

Cover Design: Elizabeth Maines

Printed in the USA on acid-free paper.
Order online: www.finishinglinepress.com
also available on amazon.com

Author inquiries and mail orders:
Finishing Line Press
P. O. Box 1626
Georgetown, Kentucky 40324
U. S. A.

Table of Contents

The House That Made Me 1
The Cusp 4
Eldest Daughter 5
La Corrida de Toros 7
After Auschwitz 9
Mrs. Rifka Straussman 11
Rabbi Mendel Straussman 13
Benjamin (Benjy) Strass 14
Zhou Ling 16
Girl's Song 17
Quartet 19
Party Girl 21
My Last Schmuck 22
In Defense of Poesy 24
Morning After 25
The Pang of All the Partings 26
Love, New and Old 28
What We Talk About 29
Honeymoon Eyes 30
I, Edith, Take You Clive 31
Wife 33
Monthling 34
Five Years Alive 36
Thirteen 37
Twenty-Three 38

The House That Made Me

In this house I became me
Mostly

This white and black kitchen where Mommy baked brownies from scratch
Leaving pebbles of unsifted flour dotting the spongy chocolate
And calling me to lick the beaters clean, "don't tell your sisters, it's our secret"
Trotting to the breakfast nook, toting my prizes, one in each triumphant
Smeared fist, to the table to sit and suck, listening to her running the faucet
Washing each spoon by hand because "dishwashers are for fancy folk"

The kitchen where Mommy spent so much time, leaning on the counters,
Standing at the sink, stirring at the stove, bending into the oven,
Reaching for the highest cabinet until the stepstool was uncranked to
Help with the height she was so challenged by, the kitchen that I liked to
Sit in while she was there, soaking in the smells and the safety of her,
Doing homework at the table with the rolling chairs, just to be near her

===

To the right the small office bedroom that once held crib, rocker and baby
Last baby sister of four, sister I thought unnecessary
Told Totty off when he called with the news, locked in the bathroom, refused to see him
"Don't you think we have enough girls?! Don't bother bringing her home"
Then my ten year old being bowled over by the newborn she and
No more need of a brother—I became the one who walked with her in the nights

In the room the antique wooden dresser that held drawer after drawer of
Pink, folded just so, tiny padded footy pajamas and daisy onesies that
I insisted on shopping my very own self with cash that they gave me
To appease for the unexpected extra sister that came home to live,
But they both soon realized as I did that the seven pounds of squalling
Powdered and pampered pink fluff was the perfectest gift ever

===

Down the hall their cool blue bedroom with two twin beds, one for each
Parent who let us crawl between their blankets some mornings when
They didn't feel like talking to each other and from there
He rose up one Shabbos afternoon from his nap stormy and
Ferocious because of our noise and reddened our rumps with
Finger stripes that we still talk about twenty years later "remember when…"

Their bedroom, with the door usually shut but opened just enough for us
To peek inside one morning to watch in horror the blood that pooled on
his bed
And streamed from his nose in bright rivers and stained his shirt a sickening
Scarlet as he lay, back arched, pressing drenched wads of tissue to the tide
As she sat on the bed holding boxes of Kleenex in one hand and the waste
Basket in the other, whispering to us four crowded in the door "it's all okay"

===

On the left my old room and our names scratched into the wood of the
Red and white sheeted bunk beds, I on the bottom bunk and she
On top with her hand stretched down in between the wall and the bed
Reaching for my fingertips that she pulled up to tease and play with
Just as I turned ten, then she was twelve and she made up
Games and dressed in filmy scarves and I always had to be the boy

The bunk bed that we used as haven from Mommy's slipper when she
Chased us round the room tripping on the stuffed bears that we tossed carefully
To the floor when we knew she'd be after us to bare our bottoms for the
Furious spanking that inevitably never happened because she couldn't climb
The ladder to the top bunk where we shrank, quaking with laughter,
But eventually she too collapsed into heaving peals at her failure to flog us

===

Next door the heavy dining room, oak breakfront and clawed table legs
Silver everything stacking the glass shelves, lace curtains peeking behind musty velvet
Brown and gold swirled carpet, a room for Friday night Shabbos *tish* and for guests
That Totty entertained when he was unhappy with Mommy's moods
He had shul friends over for Talmud talk and seltzer and murmuring while
She spent hours playing handheld Tetris splitting unsalted peanuts from their shells

The dining room was where we rarely dined, just a room that looked
A certain way, stately and stale, but we used it anyway to hide in secretly
During quiet games we invented to take up the time on weekend afternoons
As we tried to reconceive the room happier and louder, a room for us,
A room that taught the littlest one to walk when we tied the pink crocheted scarf
Round her fat middle and let go laughing when she wasn't looking behind her

This is the house that made me
Somewhat

The Cusp

layers
like nesting *matryoshka* dolls,
elaborately painted
meticulously decorated
charming, ornamental.
Without obscuring within,
art as life and so on
a spit-shined toy, collectible figurine
her father carefully handcrafted
to gift a prospective bridegroom
oohs and aahs
flowers and fairy tales
she's eighteen, almost
almost old enough to leave
almost young enough to cry about it
dig deep enough if you care to find
the true daughter, the real sister, the genuine granddaughter
the smallest girl masquerading as the largest
woman

Eldest Daughter

For the first twenty-one years of her life,
She made herself into the quintessential conformist,
Toeing the line as parents and neighbors and rabbis demanded,
Even though it killed her.

When they led her into the elegant living room in March of her eighteenth year
And introduced her to the boy she would marry later that summer,
Quick on the heels of her high school graduation,
She smiled at them as her heart splintered into a million shards.

When she cried, they took her into the dark den with its imposing paneling
And opened ten different yellowing tomes and pointed,
Trying to convince her, first subtly then severely, that it would be best to do as they said
Because love is overrated and contentment will come in time.

When her son was born she was eighteen and she hated him for stealing her youth,
As she hated her father for stealing her hair that they forced her to shave
After the wedding, as she hated her mother for wielding that razor and not fighting
For her, even though she knew her mother had survived the same charade.

When she craved a college education, she took a receptionist job instead,
And she envied other women behind the wheel while they forbade her a license,
And she hid the TV in the microwave box so no one would see how wayward
She'd become, and she did everything they told her with gall in her gut.

When she wanted some independence, they forced her onto her back
Because they wanted babies. And so she had three and loathed the entire messy business,
And they thought her tears were from the onions she dutifully grated for every Shabbos kugel,
And they thought the knife nicks and cuts among the potato peelings were all incidental.

But when her sister approached her eighteenth year, snarling and spitting,
Tossing her glossy tresses, fighting back fiercely, then driving off
Into freedom, she swallowed the little white pills
That finally killed her.

La Corrida de Toros

Father is...
Taurus
Heavy coarse thick-hide bull
Powerful hunched massive shoulders strain against black coat, collar up—
film noir villain
Lowered horns, lowering brow under shadowy black hat
Bitter steam, acid anger flare from seething nostrils above unshaven
jutting chin
Ears billow self-righteously
Clouded critical brown eyes see faint flashes of the red flag, red flag

Paws the ground, impatient snorts
Sees the red flag in strange corners
Finds a red flag in all comers
Hears the *matador* in his sleep, feels the sticking stinging *banderillas*
in his side
Hears the cheering jeering crowd egging him on
His bullring, his Pamplona where he flees some, chases others
It's July all his life, praying to San Fermin,
Seeing only red—my way, highway, red sashes amid the white of the runners

In his neighbors he sees taunting white-clad devils in scarlet sashes
       running hissing
until he is penned in panting
In his children he sees the slim elegant velvet breeches of professional
torturers
       jabbing stabbing
until the blood streams down his flanks
until he turns on them and gores
until he leaves them for dead, his enemies

Father becomes…
Grandfather
Precious awaited child soothes wounds, smoothes scars
The bull rests, breathing heaving deep
    calmed quieted
    subdued stilled
Years weigh lightly now
He has run his course

After Auschwitz

I am vague I am hazy I am indistinct

I am bodiless—
but my black Romani blood river runs
boils and bubbles and
pushes up Piotr's daisies
I am faceless—
but my non-Aryan features glow searing hot
my crippled mouth and communist eyes
coal to cinder
fuel to Himmler's furnaces
the fog of my Jewish bones
blurs Wladyslaw's farmhouse
my homosexual tongue a licking lapping flame
a hideous gape, a burning yawning mask
my embers smolder in the wake of the Zyklon B
that fumigated my lungs
and left me breathless, voiceless, mute.
Silent.

...so I am nameless...
I am vague I am hazy I am indistinct

Write me, Paul Celan
    —your neighbor from Czernowitz
Write me, Nelly Sachs
    —your neighbor from Berlin
Write me, Miklós Radnóti
    —your neighbor from Budapest

Give me a body and fill me in and grant me life.
Birth me—
for oblivion awaits
Birth me—
lest I disappear
from the awareness of humanity
into the amnesia of history
…vapor and ash…

Adorno was wrong—there must be poetry.
Write me.

Mrs. Rifka Straussman

You see me now in this frayed old photograph toned in sepia,
My tentatively perfect smile outlined in rich earthy gloss,
My gypsy-black eyes fixed sideways on an absent lover,
My felt hat tilted on top of my sleek dark chignon,
Round my neck the spotless high collar of my single holiday dress.
You see hopeful happy youth.

You do not see the wasted horror I became shortly
After the roundup and deportation in the village square—
After that surreal ride in the sealed cattle car on rails—
After they stripped me and shaved me and nearly showered me—
After they seared the blue number into my very soul.

You do not see the wretched wanderer I became shortly
After the Red Army liberated us shrunken scavengers and set us ravenous
To fight our own bodies to keep the single swallow of solid food down,
And afterward begin the grim search in hometowns and across seas
For the remains of the families.

You do not see the stubborn survivor I became shortly
After returning to the rubble that had been home and seeing
How they'd stolen my everything—
And how there was nothing and no one left for me in raped Berlin—
And how the only path out of living death was rebirth.

You do not see the resolute wife and mother I became shortly
After I married a long-ago neighbor who'd smelled the smoke
Of his daughter turned to cinder even as the stench
Of his wife's charred corpse still flooded his flesh.
And despite them—and to spite them—
We raised six perfect children in the haven of New York.

You do not see the frayed old woman I became
As the years became decades and the nightmares faded in frequency
Until that September morning, staring at the screen with incredulous eyes,
I watched the mighty towers crumple to their knees amid roiling clouds of ash,
A scene that wrenched me into a new reality, Hitler triumphant,
And I had to fight the terrifying urge to call my grown children
To gather and flee.

Rabbi Mendel Straussman

Six children are my life's success story—six,
All with their offspring trailing like ducklings in a row...
Pride and honor follow me now in the dusk of my life.
Neighbors, regal in black frock coats and fur *shtreimels* on their heads,
Nod and smile when they see me relax on my ramshackle porch
On sunny Shabbos afternoons with my tousled grandchildren gamboling at my feet.
"Nu, Reb Mendel, how are you feeling today?" I hear at my front door endlessly
From concerned friends with shared old-age maladies and common histories, and
"I baked you some *babka* today" from buxom middle-aged *hausfraus* in kerchiefs awry...
An idyllic picture, is it not?

I thank the Almighty that He chose to guide me through my twilight this way,
Granting me succor and solace through my devoted family.
But this gentle scene masks the tragic truths of my younger years:
The slaughtered wife and child who left no memoriam
Save the numbered brand burned into the baggy skin of my old man's arm—
Later, the loved seventh child who became *a shandeh far di mishpuchah*,
Disgraced his family when he turned his back on all we held close and
Wedded and bedded that Communist *shiksa* and begot foreign children,
Then didn't understand how his mother could deny her Benjy—
My wife's temporary insanity following the attacks on the towers
That convinced her she was reliving the Third Reich—
All make up the mosaic of an oppressive past but thankfully
Cannot dim the exuberant delight and tender repose I've found
Only once my body has bent and my beard has blanched and
The rotund apple-cheeks and sparkling smiling eyes of my baby grandchildren
Laugh up at me from their favorite perch on my trembling arthritic knees...

Benjamin (Benjy) Strass

This gathering is typical of family wedding parties:
Bride and groom clasp each other, happily paralyzed as
Parents and in-laws and trailers—on vamp for the photographer and inevitably
Someone's eyes are captured closed and someone else's kid now forever wails…

This is the bride's extended family, extended all the way from
Chinatown and Sunset Park and Flushing, little Fujianese ghettos.
With a single exception,
Each of these twenty four people blends seamlessly into the Asian tapestry—
Women sheathed in crimson silk cheongsams
Sporting sleek raven knots at their napes,
Men solemn in black and white with a splash of scarlet tied at their necks,
Black hair polished to a glossy finish,
Gamely waiting for that next glass of something stirring…

The single exception is the groom—myself—
The anomaly in this ocean of inclined eyes—
The groom who was raised to fear God and follow the ancient law
That He presented to Moses on two stone tablets at Mount Sinai—
Who was strictly raised to wear black hat and white shirt and pray thrice daily,
Squint at the Talmud and swing his fringed *tzitzis*,
Separate milk and meat and rest on Shabbos…

But I ultimately found God not fearsome and the law too ancient—
Moses dead and buried and the stone tablets taxing—
The black hat hot and the daily prayers dreary—
The Talmud tiresome and the *tzitzis* unwieldy—
I discovered milk and meat delicious together and that it was
More restful to drive wherever on Shabbos than to walk…

I found my wonderfully exotic wife amid the teeming bustle of
Chinese humanity on 8th Avenue in Brooklyn
Where I went faithfully, weekly, to deliver my father's wholesale produce
To the restless enterprise that sums up Sunset Park.
But my faith eventually found its limits and instead
I buried myself in her and hers.

I changed my name to temper its German-Jewish tones
Without fully realizing that my fresh new moniker unfolds me as a fraud[1]
Upon reflection I admit it's true—
Life does mock my attempts to control it
And I see my Chinese children bereft of my identity,
And myself a counterfeit of the Jew I could have been.

Now my own mother refuses to acknowledge my existence,
Although I'm one of seven wished-for children
That two Auschwitz survivors fervently made and
Papa shadows Mama in her vehement denial
That I ever emerged lusty and hale from the hollow of her womb.

So.
Since at my wedding my bride wore red,
My entire family mourns me dead.

---

[1]Strass: (paste): a. a brilliant, heavy glass used for making artificial gems b. an artificial gem of this material

Zhou Ling

My wedding portrait lies.
Glamorous beguiling smiling bride wearing
wedding cheongsam of brilliant scarlet satin
embroidered in lavish glittering gold
skimming angular curves, western bridegroom's arm
loosely draping narrow silken shoulders
flanked by many far flung Fujianese cousins and by
small stooped parents who,
even arrayed in festive attire seem to
scurry and worry

I have become utterly other. Child
who daily covered her ears to quiet the din child
who daily squinted her eyes to dim the squalor child
who daily dutifully followed father to the shops
the child has become the other—
Gentile wife to Orthodox Jew
Asia, meet Europe. China, meet Germany.
Dim sum, meet *kreplach*.
Eyes, meet eyes.

I have fashioned our family.
Tiger mother to a violinist, a chemist
prominent exceptional Asians
Parent to perfection itself but who,
as daughter did her damnedest to be
the furthest from flawless and now
smooth assimilated offspring to
impossibly immigrant parents and
heretic helpmeet to reverent husband

My wedding portrait lies.
We are more alike than people imagine,
my Jewish husband and I.

Girl's Song
    (for F.M., in memoriam)

"Hashem is here, Hashem is there…"
My childhood voice sparkles with song
floating just out of earshot, just this side of consciousness,
pregnant with promise, confident of jump ropes and joy,
brunette braids bouncing against my narrow sweatered back,
skipping in clumsy penny loafers and a long navy skirt that
obscures the human girl underneath.

"…Hashem is truly everywhere…"
Bedtime stories and children's tales,
stories of great sages, tales from the Talmud.
So it was. So it shall be.
A 17th century rabbi relates the prophecy of a mother
forced to scald her daughter's bare skin into eternity.
The women bear the burden.
So it was. So it shall be.

"…up up down down…"
Up above Hashem spills angry ink onto Rorschach clouds and His
elbows erase spots leaving sparkling starlight
winking at me, promising…
Down below the cityscape unfolds
twenty stories down, twinkling bridge towers blip,
office towers alit, the mighty Hudson slips beneath the GWB.

"…right left and all around…"
All around me they are drinking and laughing, all
elbows and knees, shocking how much bare skin shows
in the dim glow of nightlife, afterlife of daytime.
To my right a half-dressed ginger waif leans heavily
bored and sleepy on the last sober man left up here.
I am the odd one. I am out.

"...*here there and everywhere...*"
Here is my chance.
Behind me, a cold husband waits for me to dip
and cleanse my impurities in the *mikvah*
before he is permitted make more babies for Hashem.
Before me, a cold gleaming city, lights and glittering lights,
jewelry box for a Jewish bride.

"...*that's where He can be found...*"
In yeshiva the boys chant "Bless You, O Lord,
for not creating us women."
In yeshiva the girls murmur "Bless You, O Lord,
for creating us according to Your will."
In yeshiva the girls are reminded that Hashem can be found
in the crook of our elbows and the turn of our ankles.

When I fall no one will notice my scandalous ankles
when my long navy skirt flips up around my waist
as I drop twenty stories down to
where Hashem will surely meet me.

Quartet

Four musicians up on the stage.
    The drummer she crashes, laughing, cymbals clashing
        relishing thumping out the thrum thrum thrum
            keeping time time time, rhythm-keeper sublime.
The cellist she sits sedate, solemn, calm
    soulful notes swirling outward
        swan lake arms dancing round the music
            seducing the sounds forth with her bow.
The violinist she cradles her baby between
    chin, shoulder, her head inclined raptly listening to
        the whispers of the instrument wooing her.
The singer she touches the audience
    through eyes closed, entranced
        throaty torch song catching notes on the mic
            slim fingers skimming the keyboard, percussive piano.

Four wives up on the stage.
    One a widow whose four boys are home and
        they remember their father, their mother's connection
            to life before the drums rekindled her spirit and
                lit again the fire inside her.
One a longtime partner in a marriage of unequals
    her music, her talent long the substance of combat,
        he blames her for escaping him into the nighttime
            of gigs and girlfriends, her cello itself sultry suggestive of
                the other woman, all curves and deep throat.
One a new mother, new wife, new person whose
    violin she cares for like the life she birthed
        and she gently caresses the body, the strings
            feather touching bow cooing, crooning.
One a divorcee whose passion for husband now
    channeled into the ivory keys that she touches so
        lovingly stroking, eliciting
            heaven on earth.

Four Orthodox women up on the stage.
   The drummer she's dressed modest, tights
      underneath demure black skirt
         curly dark wavy wig
           her look discreetly subtle but
              nothing bland about her way of
                 belting out the pounding sounds
                    walking humbly with her God but
                       a demon at her drums.
The cellist she's dressed modest, tights
   underneath flowing gypsy skirt that allows
      the bowed instrument to rest between her legs
      the single hint of the sensual being whose
         spiritual mystique is best left to imagine
            staring straight ahead, straight hair severely tied,
               her wig symbolic of her faith's constraints.
The violinist she's dressed modest, tights
   underneath long peasant skirt
      disheveled blond wig belies the
         devotion evident in her reverent
            rendition of the band's finale.
The singer she's dressed modest, tights
   underneath slim but proper pencil skirt
      leather jacket hiding skinny tank top
      punch of color at her heels
         pale loose long locks of her wig swinging
            swinging in time, in rock star rhyme
            her naked female voice
               heard by fellow females only.

Four people up on the stage.

Party Girl

Dazzling diamonds at her throat
Dangerous daggers in her smile
Dissonant discordant lifestyle.
Glittering resplendent evening gown
Gagging retching bulimic shell
Gaunt radiant perfection.
Whimsical magnetic enchanting eyes
Pernicious malignant exhaustion
Profoundly weary of the miserable war.
Surrounded by glamorous circle of darlings
Haunted by ghastly ring of demons
Gasping desiccated romantic lie.
Social niceties fallen from laughing lips
Sweet nothings whispered in bejeweled ears
Sadistic numbing nonchalance
Sarcastic nihilism rules her inner sanctum.

How long can she play the parody before the expensive paint peels and the careful varnish cracks and the counterfeit veneer crumbles and she is left naked

My Last Schmuck

I can quote Keats.
A thing of beauty, blah blah…
I can use the word "antidisestablishmentarianism"
in a sentence.
I think I know who Boutros Boutros-Ghali is.
If pressed, I might even be able to tell you.
I am a cosmopolitan bon vivant.
I am not a geek.
I am not a freak.
I do not like green eggs and ham.
I lie with consummate facility.
[I also lie with all the Hooters girls.]
I am looking for a harridan or a virago.
Willing to settle for a shrew.
Or you?
I am spiritually savvy; I positively levitate.
I am looking for my soul mate—
or a cell mate—
or a primate?
I am equally comfortable in jeans and a T
as in a tux
or in spats
or in your bedroom.
WINK WINK
[I am smoothly subtle. Haven't you noticed?]
I am successfully successful.
I am looking to write Aldous Huxley's significant sequel.
I floss.
I put the toilet seat down.
Actually, I don't.
Sometimes I'll work.
Sometimes I won't.
I am an occasional panhandler.
I am an occasional philanderer.

I am occasionally good at painting, passing gas, partying, and parting.
Especially good at parting.
Just ax my ex.
And my other ex.
I am a REAL MAN.
I see myself entirely as others see me.
Don't you see?

Ladies…your future spouse is here.

In Defense of Poesy

"Ah love, let us be true to one another"
might work on the tumbled blonde sprawled next to you
with the vacant glazed gaze and rumpled stained dress invitingly
lifted revealing creamy thighs striped with your insouciant fingertips
and bruising lips as she listens rapturously and insensibly to your
impassioned rehearsed recitation while you wait for the hushed slow sleepy
unfolding of her body beneath yours, your performance reminiscent of
one who lights candles and kindles incense only
to elicit her sweet elixir when she shows up at your door
for a night of play and waits to be
gentled under your touch

Morning After

Last night we drank ourselves into desperate darkness and now
a freight train hurtles and rips through my head
It derails in the nebulous oblivion between sex and sleep
The dawn coasts into day
weaving and dragging pleasures and shadows
mingling with sharp edges and you

We wake with hot foggy mouths heavy hesitant eyes
clinging blindly and silently to our cloaked selves
In the fragile cocoon of each other we founder and sink
into
                boundless
                                  indifference

Tell me again how I am
in the red gold glow of early light

The Pang of All the Partings

Over an appetizer of black beans and warm goat cheese I recognized your true nature
Beyond sex, food, wine and weed you do not exist
Beyond yourself you do not exist
But I remembered how we met and how we were together

How I danced to the exquisite thrumming sound of Jim Morrison
coaxing me in his perfect baritone to join his soft parade,
the soft parade in which I could passionately and singularly march,
the only sound in the world as
my limbs undulated to the languid rhythm as if they were distant, detached and floating on water

How we lay sunken on the cushions behind the wall of windows facing the ocean as the sentinel moon hovered over the midnight satin sheet of water
How the haunting strains of Pink Floyd seeped into our blood and bones until we could not distinguish between our corporeal bodies and our numbed spirits
How you set dried flowers on the tables and the walls, upside down roses in bleached colors of claret and peach…
How your shadow mingled with the scent of incense burning, gentle citrus smoke…
How the grass was sweet in our lungs as
you lit white candles in old wine bottles heavy with melted wax from other candles, other lovers

You were always one for creating atmosphere
I was always one for making you rise and howl

I tried not to notice when you climbed the stairs, carelessly
followed by the big bottomed Albanian girl in the scarlet swimsuit
who had joined the party but then remained there in your room, endlessly
Alone with you

I pretended I didn't care
I thought I didn't care
I didn't care

And that's why
I left you sixty dollars for last night's dinner
I left you in the hushed early hours before the cool creeping dawn
I left you sleeping in the tumbled white bed with the bean bag pillows facing the ocean
I left you

Love, New and Old

New love...
Her mouth stretches in an unending smile, unbidden,
ticket to transcendence
How she runs to him!
Liquid laughter bubbles at the back of her throat
She is perpetually poised at the brink of buoyancy
Her lungs catch breath in anticipation of his voice
teasing, titillating, feeding her in tender swells

Her country is lush and verdant and new and undiscovered

Before the snapping leaping flames they are entangled on the rug,
lit gently by the ruby reflection of the Merlot,
reciting verse and touching subliminally.
Impassioned tango for two, primal strains of Ravel as the *Bolero*
throbs through
Ardent arousal, slow suffuse of red desire,
blind heat of fire and warm low growl of his baritone breathing on her
sheer living skin

Then a cautious cooling, anti-climax,
slow steady breathing of his spent form turned from her in sleep
Stately *pavanne*, solemn and staunch, ceremony and distance
govern their interplay
Ember and ash in the grate, beer and remote in his hand,
lit eerily by the flickering blue glow,
he is nodding and twitching over the paper in his lap
and yawning subliminally.

Her world is gray and arid and used and past its prime

Her lungs catch breath in apprehension of his evening mood
spinning her day down into a swirling widening gyre
She is perpetually poised at the edge of escape
Salty sentiment tightens her throat, threatens her careful composure
Yet she stays with him...
Her mouth stretches in a fixed smile, forced, passport to peace
Old love.

What We Talk About

What we talk about
when we talk about
everything is
what we talk about
when we talk about
nothing,
except sex.
What we talk about
when we talk about
sex is
what we talk about
when we talk about
power.
Except power
is the thing
we talk about
when we don't talk about
you and me.
And that's the way it's always been
and that's the way it always will be.
Because we don't know
how to talk about
not talking about
you and me.

Honeymoon Eyes

Everything is filtered through honeymoon eyes.
The Piazza San Marco, its squabble of pigeons and
tourists, a little bit of Italy.

David Gilmour, pinkly lit
through misty sheets of summer storm sounds
comfortably numb as he
hums mightily to the crowd
where we stand.
Us. And them is everyone.

Black and blue
we later found to be
the colors of that evening,
when our sweet Aurora was conceived in
more than thought,
more bacchanal than beloved,

straight from a Veronese painting, the kind
the Doge lived inside.
Brilliant luminous hues of viridian, cerulean, scarlet
blood, mine and yours awash with wine,
giddy with cannabis and canals and cannoli.

Me in my dangerous blue dress and you reveling
with me at the Caffe Paradiso.

I, Edith, Take You Clive

What stirs Edith to begin writing
early early wee hours
staring down the bottom of the bottle
of Glenlivet that she stirs
every few minutes wondering
is it worth it
to drain the last last drop drink
clink a fifth a fifth
the bottle was many fifths full before
the sun sank.
Clive watches a coyote golden eyed
slink pad footed over leaf beds
the desiccated leaves of
an early autumn leaves
descend silent landing
winter fall its paws steal
up the hill Clive cups his chin
ragged coal cracked fingernails
chapped palms four fingers hold his
cigarette loose chafing the gold band
the ember is a halo
he watches the turkey strut strut gobble gobble
does it even know Thanksgiving is next week
next week around the corner
its day is coming
the turkey half its size last year
still struts when it hurries
it thinks of a gazelle
the coyote and the turkey
padding strutting
Edith watches Clive through streaked glass panes
standing legs akimbo on the porch
so dark he's pitch
breathing steam into the winter fall
their boy says watch me steam the air
I'm breathing

Clive's glowing ember between his fingers
shimmers in the black air
as he watches a coyote gleam.
Edith writes Clive.
She drinks him and she writes him and she glimmers
in the crystal whisky.

Wife

That's all she really is, someone's property, a *wife*,
That sole identity defines her narrow life.
What she shops, whom she meets, what she spends, where she goes,
All must be accounted for, down to all she does.
Her reality is misery. Wretched female,
Lives a dismal existence, accursed and stale.
She and that veritable stranger, her husband,
Teeter on their marriage's raw jagged cusp and
He treats her with coldness, cruelty, contempt,
Efficiently thwarting her meager attempts
To reconcile with him, to make him love her.
But she tends, in her oppressive timidity, to hover,
Irking him 'til he lashes out and destroys
Her shy pretty ways that once were his joys.
She thinks that their only conceivable hope,
The one saving grace that would allow her to cope
With their unraveling bond, would be a baby—
Her single constant thought, that someday maybe
She'd be ever redefined, as someone's mother.
Then she'd feel potent enough to be other
Than the sniveling timid creature she feels like with him.
But the specialists hand her a life sentence grim:
Her womb is too feeble—she'd never conceive.
She exists, endlessly, in search of reprieve—
Perhaps the next pedigree she tries to consult
Would incredibly predict a different result.
No matter. Her pitiful life is already
Fashioned by bitterness, unceasing and steady.
The pungent streams of disillusionment and doubt
That plague her incessantly are not all about
Being barren. Her blanched translucent face,
Her slender trembling hands and sad poignant grace,
All herald defeat, though she drifts in denial.
A baby won't save her—or them—by a mile.

Monthling

at one month you were tiny
a silent speck in the gray light and dark graininess
of the ultrasound
indistinguishable
from all other sprinkles in the speckled galaxy
of my womb
I wanted you to be a girl speck
right there in the blurred organic moonscape
of my womb
I had visions of ruffled pink gingham and glitter

at four months you were rounded and shadowy
a piebald balloon stick figure
your parts waxing and waning as
you jerked away from the probe—I could see
your alien head haloed in white
your puppet leg floating bodiless, bloodless
miniature bones shaping a miniature human

at eight months you were enormous
filling the screen with dappled shades
of gray and white and black
hazy and stark white ridgy rib cage
inside a cavernous dark ball
filling the room with the insistent mechanical whoosh
of your heartbeat
there was no fear, there was no joy, there was no me,
there was only you

at one month you were tiny
your gossamer breath fluttering the butterfly wings
on my arm hairs. Every night I sneaked out of my marriage bed
to hold my breath, to watch your pink rib cage rise and fall
ebb and flow, to inhale the downy silk of your nape
to smell your milky almond mouth and feel the warm damp heft
of your bottom
to listen for the mewling that always came right before
you needed me

Five Years Alive

Sufi whirlwind dervish of my life, spinning spinning fever giddy, energy embodied—body in motion, moving the very breath of being, consuming the very chaos, overtaking the very air. HE IS VERY. Spirited superlative, nothing by halves, buoyant remarkable alive, playful puppy inside of a boy bounding scampering nose-nose kissing, compelling. crossing my lines, perseverating. pushing my boundaries, punishing rousing yet still my very own lovable Looney Tunes Tazmanian devil, fiery haloed blue-eyed—angel actually, enchanting smile melting a golden pathway through anger and annoyance, exciting—exasperating—extraordinary exultant Tom Sawyer, chieftain of mischief, charming disarming testing chancing dancing to his private drumbeat, delicious adorable teachers' darling loving laughing heartfelt boy hurtling through swinging doors singing…in out out in out out out…
this is how we define magnificent boyhood—
a miracle, a marvel, a maelstrom.
infuriating invincible frenetic
kinetic thrilling and thrilled
sometimes vexing, always vital
always vibrant always always
The Incredible Dash!
racing speeding
bolting flying
why walk
when you
can run
like
him

Thirteen

man-boy
mass of anomaly
twin tentacles of frustration and serenity
uneasy harmony of wit and travesty
chafing shimmering humor
simmering rebellion
renegade wisdom, barely contained
rearing up in outrage and mirth
illuminating ideas
eggshell ego
shifting crowding warring thoughts
cloaked tentative sparkling smile
careful careless drama
soulful delightful warmth
solemn sweet prince
edgy misty lovely prickly simply—
son

Twenty-Three

dimming youth, dawning maturity
the thirteen year old has aged ten years…
A decade on, he's developed into
what the world believes is a man
balancing the act of life
as an Olympian
diving into the deep
confident of the trophy at the finish
cautiously courageous
brilliantly brazen
future-focused yet sometimes
haunted by ghosts of failures past but
bearing the burden, a Stoic at heart
steadfast strong singularly keen
eyes on the prize
grateful for his myriad gifts
gracious glorious quixotic human
self-determined dedicated disciplined
his mother's champion above all
a free and nimble exploring mind—
an adventurer.
dauntless laughing radiant resolute—
a contender.

Still in all,
I believe it will take his lifetime to become
a man.
And I hold my applause.

www.ingramcontent.com/pod-product-compliance
Lightning Source LLC
LaVergne TN
LVHW041551070426
835507LV00011B/1038